GW00493029

Got those
POSITION
BLUES?

9 jazzy pieces for violin and piano in
2nd, 3rd and 4th positions

---

9 jazzige Stücke für Violine und Klavier in der
zweiten, dritten und vierten Lage

Edward Huws Jones

FABER ff MUSIC

Got those position blues? brings a fresh approach to third (and second and fourth) position, with a series of progressive pieces in a lively jazz idiom.

For young violinists third position can be a formidable technical hurdle. Many students encounter it for the first time in the approach to Grade 3, a stage when an up-tempo jazz or pop style will be particularly welcome. With its strong rhythmic element, the jazz idiom powers the pieces along, creating a momentum which helps to overcome left hand problems.

One of the features of the pieces is the use of finger patterns which repeat on different strings and/or in different positions. The techniques of learning positions have therefore been incorporated into the musical language of the pieces. Rather than employ arbitrary positions and shifts simply to make a technical point, the positions and shifts suggested are usually the most natural and effective way to play the music.

Primarily, these are pieces which young violinists *will want to play* – and which also happen to be in positions other than first. *So no more position blues!*

Got those position blues! ermöglicht einen ganz neuen Zugang zur dritten, aber auch zur zweiten und vierten Lage, mit jazzigen Stücken von fortschreitender Schwierigkeit.

Für junge Geiger ist die dritte Lage manchmal eine ziemliche technische Hürde. Viele Schüler begegnen ihr zum ersten Mal mit etwa 11 bis 13 Jahren, einem Alter, in dem lebhafte Stüke mit Anklängen von Jazz oder Pop besonders willkommen sind. Die vor allem durch Rhythmus geprägte Tonsprache des Jazz trägt den Spieler mit Schwung durch die Stücke, so daß Probleme der linken Hand leicht überwunden werden.

Eine der Besonderheiten dieser Stücke ist die Verwendung gleicher Fingersätze auf verschiedenen Saiten und/oder in verschiedenen Lagen. Die technische Erarbeitung neuer Lagen wird so musikalischer Bestandteil der neu zu erlernenden Stücke. Die in den Werken vorgeschlagenen Lagen und Lagenwechsel sind deshalb nicht einfach zur Bewältigung technischer Probleme vorgeschrieben, sondern ergeben sich als die meist naheliegendste und effektvollste Lösung zur Ausführung der Stücke.

Vor allem aber handelt es sich um Stücke, die der junge Geiger wird spielen *wollen*, Stücke, die dann eher zufällig in anderen als der ersten Lage stehen – *keine Angst vor neuen Lagen!*

© 1995 by Faber Music Ltd
First published in 1995 by Faber Music Ltd
3 Queen Square London WC1N 3AU
Cover design by Lynette Williamson
Music processed by Wessex Music Services
German translations by Dorothee Göbel
Printed in England by Halstan and Co Ltd
All rights reserved

ISBN 0 571 51534 7

1. Got Those 3rd Position Blues?

EDWARD HUWS JONES

© 1995 by Faber Music Ltd.

This music is copyright. Photocopying is illegal.

4

2. Hard Rock Cafe

Heavy rock tempo ♩ = 88

3. L. A.

4. Miles Away

5. Banana Skin

6. Open Sesame

tempo I

7. Looking Sheepish

8. Second Stride

Moderate rock tempo ♩ = 108

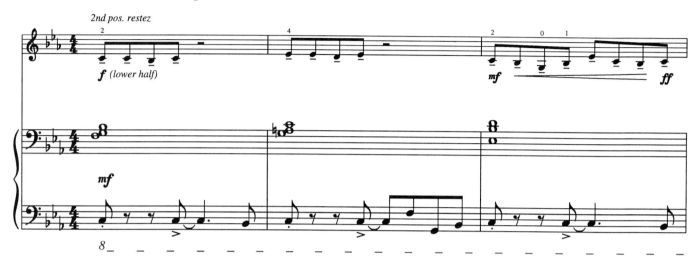

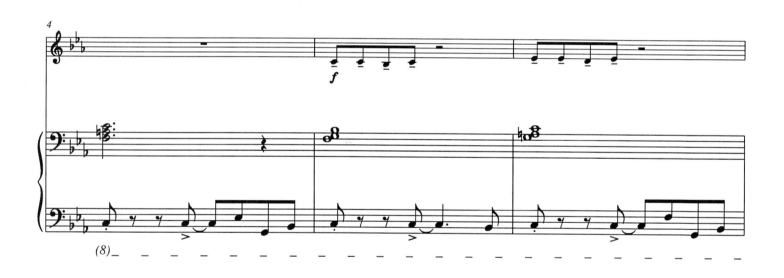

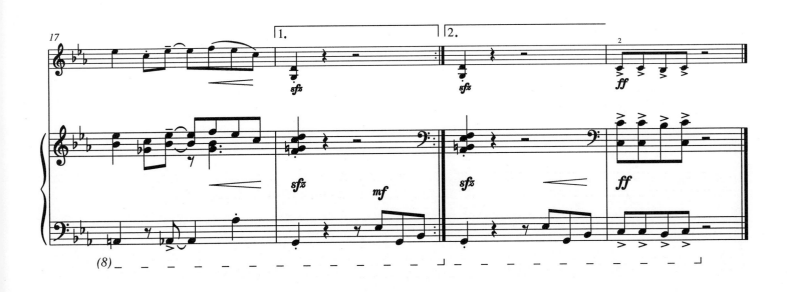

9. Adrienne